AF326532

After the Rain

A guided journal of discovering passion and unleashing purpose

Deondriea Cantrice

Way, Inc
Prosper, TX

Dedication

To everyone that is entering into or weathering their storm. *After the Rain* you will see the sunrise and the beauty of the rainbow. Remain encouraged and let your purpose be your passion.

Introduction

You have taken the first step towards discovering passion and unleashing purpose. I am so excited that you have decided to walk in the fullness of life. You may be asking yourself, *"I have read a multitude of books, attended conferences across the country and I still find that I'm lost, stuck, or bound to someone or something; how is this journal going to transition me from where I am to where I desire to be?"* Healing is an internal process and in order for you to begin to truly heal, you must acknowledge the storm or what has happened and how it has affected you.

In life, rain serves as a metaphor for the storms that exist in our lives. Just as the heavens open and surrender their moisture, we also face moments when our lives appear cloudy and turbulent. The pattering raindrops mirror the tears, the outpourings of joy, pain, or reflection that all souls experience. And in the same way that no two raindrops are identical, each life storm is unique, characterized by its own intensity, duration, and impact.

A rainstorm, however fierce, eventually recedes, followed by clear skies or a gentle drizzle. Similarly, human struggles, no matter how overwhelming, are transient. After each downpour, there emerges a period of calm, clarity, or even growth. The saturated earth, having absorbed every drop, becomes fertile ground for new life. After our personal storms, we often find ourselves more resilient, having absorbed lessons that prepare us for the next unpredictable gust of wind.

Yet, it's essential to remember that rain, though at times perceived as melancholy, plays a vital role in the circle of life. It nourishes, rejuvenates, and transforms. It's the harbinger of life in many ecosystems, signaling rebirth and renewal. Similarly, the storms in our lives, though daunting, often lead to periods of immense personal growth, introspection, and transformation. They water the seeds of change, facilitating the blooming of new perspectives and wisdom.

In embracing this correlation, we recognize a universal truth: Life storms, like rain, are natural, inevitable, and integral to the human experience. Both shape the world and the individual, carving valleys of understanding and raising mountains of strength.

After the Rain will challenge you to look within yourself to uncover the hurts, disappointments, and events that have left you scarred, scared or cynical. Once you recognize the triggering events or pivotal moments that cause you to withdraw, breakdown, or shut down, it will be easy to rediscover your purpose and where your passion lies. This journal was created with the intent to help you work through the barriers that are keeping you in bondage and obstructing your communication with your internal voice.

The storms of life are inevitable; the key is in learning how to weather the storm and understand the purpose of the rain so that you can continue to live, laugh, and love after the clouds have disappeared. *After the Rain* is merely a tool that will help guide you to discovering your purpose. There are no quick fixes or any easy answers, but you will find that the reward is greater than the work. I crafted this journal for those who are committed to making a change in their lives. Your commitment, desire, and continued discipline will predicate your level of success.

After the Rain is your opportunity to be intimate with your thoughts and have positive self-talk. You must be transparent with yourself as you explore your thoughts and feelings. Don't simply reflect on your life, inspect your choices, and evaluate your actions.

As you read through the pages and begin to pen your inner thoughts, recite affirmations and jot down your feelings about the quotes. Remember your storms will never define you, but they will refine you!

I send positivity and blessings your way as you begin your journey down the path of wholeness. ~Deondriea Cantrice

The Rain

*M*ost people do not enjoy the rain because it seems to show up at the most inopportune times, such as the day we wash our cars or the one time we failed to pack an umbrella. The same holds true for our personal storms! It seems that the skies darken, and we feel the first raindrop of despair when we are not prepared. Although we are not always prepared for or very welcoming of the rain, it has its benefits. In understanding our own purpose, it's important to understand the purpose of the storms in our lives.

Let's explore a few benefits of rain. Growing up in the Midwest, it seemed like the more rain we had the faster the grass would grow. Rain is a part of the circle of life. It causes things to grow, to reproduce and to become revitalized. As you look back over your life during your storms you may discover that you regained strength, grew closer to those in your circle, and maybe even added people, a new way of thinking or insight into your life that has enhanced your life in some capacity.

I remember as a little girl, we would play with colored chalk on the sidewalks. After the rain there was no sign that little girls ever played hopscotch on the pavement. A good rain washes away dirt and debris. It exposes things and people that you thought were lost. Or it unearths and exposes things and people for what and who they are. As you reflect over your life, who showed up? Who showed their true colors?

There's nothing like a summer day after the rain. Somehow the temperature seems cooler, and the humidity has subsided. As it rains in your life, situations and emotions have time to cool, to die down and bring balance as it replenishes.

As the skies clear, the rainbow appears reminding us of the promises of God. We have clarity and hope. As you look at the rainbow, it's a range of vibrant colors that has no end. But legend has it that at the end of the rainbow there is gold! Think of yourself as that rainbow, which rises with beauty above the chaos of life and ends with a reward of gold, a substance that is created through refinement!

During your storms, be still, take shelter, dance, or weather it because *After the Rain* you will be replenished, rise and have clarity.

Rain is a part of the circle of life, the rain naturally causes things to grow, to reproduce and to become revitalized. The damp air and the dark skies were not fun, but the tulips and perennials that blossomed from the rain were amazing. The bright colors of the flowers were the result of Mother Nature's watering. Smelling the flowers during the soft summer breezes made those cloudy days worthwhile.

A good rain washes away dirt and debris. I remember as a little girl, we would draw on the sidewalks with colored chalk. We would turn the sidewalk into our canvas to practice drawing, spelling, and playing games, if we made a mistake there was no way to erase our errors, until it rained of course. *After the Rain* there was no sign that little girls ever played hopscotch or drew on the pavement, using chalk pastels as their guide.

The rain exposes or unearths things that we believe were lost. In the Midwest we often endured violent storms. The strong winds and hard rains would beat up the soil and displace some of the grassy areas. I can remember going outside to find trash and treasures, everything from discarded potato chips to coins and small toys. Yes, we would be expected to pick up the trash that was discovered, but we also were able to keep the loose change that we found. Also, I noticed that the rain only shifted what was loose or not sturdy. The rain would knock over empty trash cans, but the dumpsters were unmoved.

The rain replenishes what has been depleted. The year I moved to Dallas; the lake levels were very low because of the drought. Boats were docked, and swimming was prohibited because it had been more than 80 days since the city had experienced any rain fall. One day it began to rain, and it seemed to rain daily for more than 30 consecutive rain days restoring our lakes to safe levels. With the rainfall, the flowers blossomed, and the grass grew in the most beautiful green anyone could imagine.

The next time life presents a storm, remember the hidden symphony of growth playing in the background. For After the Rain, the world always seems a little fresher, a little more vibrant, and so do we.

After the Rain is more than just a phrase; it encapsulates the transformative essence of nature and self. This upcoming collection of writing prompts seeks to explore the rejuvenation, clarity, and growth that often follows life's storms. Just as the world is reborn, washed clean, and draped in a new light after a rainstorm, our internal landscapes to undergo shifts after moments of turbulence. Through these prompts, embark on a journey of introspection and discovery, allowing the metaphor of rain to guide you through your emotions, memories, and aspirations. Let each question serve as a raindrop, nourishing the seeds of self-awareness and paving the way for personal growth.

Describe the current challenge you're facing as if it were a storm. What does it look, sound, and feel like?

____

____

____

____

____

____

Who or what did the rain wash away?

____

____

____

____

____

____

List three unexpected positive outcomes or lessons that have emerged from this difficult period.

____

____

____

____

Reflect on a past challenge you overcame. How did you do it, and how can you apply those strategies now?

____

____

____

____

____

____

____

Write down all the emotions you're feeling, without judgment. Now, write a comforting response to each one.

____

____

____

____

____

____

Visualize a moment in the future when you've weathered this storm. What does your life look like, and how do you feel?

____

____

____

____

____

____

Identify three resources or tools (e.g., friends, books, meditation) that can help you navigate this challenging period.

____

____

____

____

____

If you were to predict the course of this challenge, how do you see it unfolding, and how would you like it to resolve?

____

____

____

____

____

____

____

Write a letter to your current self from your future self, offering advice on how to navigate this storm.

What small, daily actions can you take to make this storm a bit easier or more manageable?

____

____

____

____

____

____

How has this challenge forced you to grow or change? What new strengths or insights have you discovered?

____

____

____

____

____

____

Even in tough times, there's something to be grateful for. List five things you're thankful for right now.

____

____

____

____

____

Reflect on any necessary changes or adjustments you need to make in your life to better handle or move past this storm.

____

____

____

____

____

Describe a place, real or imagined, where you feel completely safe and sheltered from the storm. What makes it so comforting?

Nature often seems refreshed and renewed after a storm. How would you like to emerge from this challenge refreshed or renewed?

What did the rain teach you about yourself?

____

____

____

____

____

____

____

What are the major storms that you have experienced in your life?

____

____

____

____

____

____

What was the result of the storm? What did you lose?

____

____

____

____

____

____

____

How did it affect you? What did you feel?

____

____

____

____

____

____

What did learn from the storm?

Who or what serves as your beacon of hope during tough times? Describe their influence on your spirit and mindset.

What did the storm revitalize in your life?

PURPOSE

*E*veryone and everything around us point to a specific PURPOSE. The challenge is understanding purpose. The word has become so common place that I believe it has lost its validity and power. Purpose is defined as the reason for which something or someone exists, or is made, used, or to possess an intended or desired result, aim or goal for oneself, to resolve to do something. The challenge is identifying and understanding purpose not only for ourselves, but the purpose of the things we have experienced and endured.

Purpose, like a compass needle, quietly and incessantly points us towards our vision. It's the silent force that awakens us, a beacon in the darkest of nights, guiding us towards meaning even when the path is shrouded in uncertainty. Every soul seeks it, consciously or otherwise, for purpose is what fills the spaces between heartbeats, making each thud resonate with significance. It is not merely an external goal, but an inner calling that transforms mundanity into art, silence into symphonies.

Purpose is the alchemy that turns struggles into stories and experiences into wisdom. While the vast expanse of life might seem random and chaotic, it is our purpose that weaves threads of coherence, creating a tapestry rich with intent. It reminds us that we are not mere driftwood carried by the tides of time, but sailors navigating its vast oceans, with destinations waiting to be reached. Every breath, every step, every moment becomes more profound when infused with purpose. And in its pursuit, we discover that true purpose is not just about reaching a destination, but also about cherishing the journey and evolving with every bend in the road.

Although two people may be doing the same thing at the same time does not mean that they have the same purpose. Your purpose is as unique as you are, so never compare yourself to others. As you give yourself permission to live, walk in your own power, and forgive yourself for your past, you will discover your purpose.

As you begin your journey through the process, unleash your passion, define your priorities, and focus on purpose. Give yourself permission to live, walk in your own power, forgive yourself, and remove those self-imposed limitations, you will discover the life that you desire.

Purpose is a multifaceted gem, born from a delicate interplay of various elements that shape our human experience. At its core lies passion, the fiery energy that ignites our drive. Coupled with understanding, it allows us to recognize the profound nuances of our journey, ensuring our path aligns with our inner truths. Reasons serve as the foundational pillars, justifying our choices and actions, while priorities help us to filter out the noise, highlighting what truly matters. Opportunities present doors, some hidden, some evident, urging us to knock and explore. Our self-esteem acts as the mirror, reflecting our worth and potential back to us, fortifying our belief in our capabilities. Lastly, expectations, both our own and those of others, subtly contour the trajectory of our purpose, serving as both challenges and motivators. Together, these elements coalesce, creating a purpose that is as unique as a fingerprint, guiding our life's narrative.

P.U.R.P.O.S.E in reality is the combination of Passion, **U**nderstanding, **R**easons, **P**riorities, **O**pportunities, **S**elf-Esteem and Expectations! It's time to unleash your PURPOSE!

What is my **Passion**?

____

____

____

____

____

I **U**nderstand the impact that my passion has.

____

____

____

____

____

What are my **R**easons or motives that drive my desire to make a change in my life?

____

____

____

____

____

____

What are my **P**riorities? And, Why?

____

____

____

____

____

____

What **O**pportunities can I create in my life?

In what condition is my **S**elf-Esteem? How do I see myself?

What are my **Expectations** concerning success?

____

____

____

____

____

____

____

Looking at your responses, what do you believe your purpose is?

____

____

____

____

____

____

Have you been walking in your purpose? Why or why not?

____

____

____

____

____

____

Do you foresee any challenges that will prevent you from walking in your purpose?

____

____

____

____

____

____

With the information that you have, you can begin formulating a PURPOSEFUL PLAN for your life.

____

____

____

____

____

____

____

____

____

____

I AM pursuing my passion with purpose on purpose!

Establishing Goals

A person can't be pushed towards their goal if they are not willing to take the first step.

There are so many things that we know we need to do, things we should do and of course, the things that we want to do. How do you make it all happen? We set GOALS! By setting goals it becomes easier to manage our time, recognize our priorities and facilitate our actions.

When establishing your goals, make them realistic, measurable and attainable. Do not set yourself up for failure by setting goals that are almost impossible to achieve! For example, it is unrealistic to believe that you can lose 150lbs in 60 days.

Do not set your goals too low either. It is not a stretch for you to lose 15 pounds in 90 days. The goals that you establish should challenge you to be creative and grow. They should prompt a lifestyle change or at least a change in your thought pattern.

You can work on one goal at a time, but no more than three. It is important that you plan how you will accomplish your goals. Are your goals designed specifically for you? Remember, it takes desire, discipline, and commitment to successfully reach your goal. There are 4 simple steps to help ensure your success.

Be specific and assign a deadline-What? By when?

It is easy to overlook something when it's ambiguous or lacks a due date. Instead of saying:

"I need more clients" try *"I will have 10 new clients by the end of the year."*

Develop a strategy-What? How?

Often, it's not our goals that are unattainable, we just fail to create a strategy that is in alignment with a plan to achieve those goals. It doesn't matter how specific your goal is, if you don't have a plan to implement it, you won't achieve your goal.

- What tools or resources will you need?
- What is the process or approach to achieve the goal?

It is important that you plan how you will accomplish your goals. What tools will you need? Do you have access to the tools that you need? Are your goals realistic? Are your goals designed for you, or are they the image that someone else has made for you? Remember, circumstances do not define who you are, but they can define your strengths. It takes desire and commitment to successfully reach your goal.

As I strive to achieve my goals, I will make sure that I reward myself during the process to build my confidence. Rewards are important because they will give me a sense of achievement. Rewards will also keep me disciplined and motivated. I understand my rewards don't have to be monetary, but they have to be meaningful. As I reach milestones towards accomplishing my goals, I will give myself the following rewards:

I will reward myself with

___________________________ if I

_________________________________.

I will reward myself with

___________________________ if I

_________________________________.

I will reward myself with

___________________________ if I

_________________________________.

MY GOAL(S)

Goal #1

____

____

____

What are the benefits that I will receive if I achieve this goal?

____

____

____

What impact will failing to achieve this goal have on my life?

____

____

____

____

How do I plan to achieve this goal?

____

____

____

____

____

____

What are potential barriers or behaviors that
may hinder me from achieving this goal?

____

____

____

____

____

____

What inner strengths can I use to achieve this
goal?

____

____

____

____

____

____

____

What resources will I need to accomplish this
goal?

____

____

____

____

____

It doesn't matter who's for you, with you or against you.
YOU have to focus and pursue your goals.

Goal #2

____

____

____

What are the benefits that I will receive if I
achieve this goal?

____

____

____

____

What impact will failing to achieve this goal
have on my life?

____

____

____

____

____

How do I plan to achieve this goal?

____

____

____

____

____

____

What are potential barriers or behaviors that
may hinder me from achieving this goal?

____

____

____

____

____

____

What inner strengths can I use to achieve this
goal?

____

____

____

____

____

____

____

What resources will I need to accomplish this
goal?

____

____

____

____

____

*I am confident enough to set goals that seem
to be out of my reach, but within my sight! ~Deondriea*

Goal #3

____

____

____

What are the benefits that I will receive if I
achieve this goal?

____

____

____

____

*You possess the power within to conquer any obstacle and
achieve every goal!*

What impact will failing to achieve this goal
have on my life?

____

____

____

____

How do I plan to achieve this goal?

What are potential barriers or behaviors that may hinder me from achieving this goal?

What inner strengths can I use to achieve this
goal?

____

____

____

____

____

____

____

What resources will I need to accomplish this
goal?

____

____

____

____

____

It doesn't matter who's for you, with you or against you.
YOU have to focus and pursue your goals.

Goal setting and affirmations are intricately intertwined, serving as the blueprint and the fuel for personal growth, respectively. Setting clear, tangible goals provides a roadmap, charting the course for our aspirations and ambitions. It gives our endeavors direction and shapes our daily actions and decisions. On the other hand, affirmations act as the motivational mantra, infusing our journey with positivity and determination. They reinforce our beliefs in our capabilities and help combat self-doubt and external challenges. By reciting and internalizing these powerful, positive statements, we constantly remind ourselves of our potential and our worth, creating a mental environment conducive to achieving our set goals.

Together, goal setting and affirmations form a potent combination, ensuring not only that we have a clear vision of where we're going but also the unwavering belief that we'll get there.

Affirmations are powerful, intentional statements that serve as anchors during life's tumultuous storms. They act as reminders of our inner strength, resilience, and innate capacity to overcome challenges. By vocalizing and internalizing these positive assertions, we reframe our mindset, replacing doubt and fear with confidence and hope. Amidst the storms and flows of life's unpredictabilities, affirmations function as a steadfast lighthouse, guiding us safely through adversity and illuminating the path towards healing and growth. Embracing affirmations is a proactive step towards weathering life's storms, ensuring we emerge not just intact, but transformed and empowered.

Time to create your own affirmations; you can start with one specific area of your life or craft as many as your heart desires. Feel free to write affirmations about ANYTHING! Think about what you would really like to change about yourself, your life, and your desires, then be confident enough to write them down, expecting the affirmations to manifest themselves in your life.

1. Your affirmation should always be in first person, to make the affirmation personal, including the words *me, myself,* or *I.*

2. Your affirmation should include positive words, avoid *can't, won't,* and *not.*

3. Include powerful words in your affirmations; use your authoritative voice with words such as *abundance, victory, success, claim* and *declare.*

4. Write your affirmation in current and future tense using words like *am, will, possess,* and *have.*

5. Write affirmations that matter to you. There is no right or wrong affirmation, nor can an affirmation be too major or too minor.

6. Create affirmations with emotion, include feeling words when necessary. Be bold, be excited, be confident!

7. Be grateful when crafting your affirmations!
    a. *I am grateful that I paid off my debt.*
    b. *I am thankful that I have unconditional love.*

8. Be specific when writing your affirmations, say exactly what you want and when.

9. It's ok to write multiple affirmations about the same thing.

What thinking patterns or perceptions would I like to change?

____

____

____

____

What circumstances would I like to improve or transform?

____

____

____

____

____

____

What experiences would I like to have?

____

____

____

____

____

____

What feelings would I like to enjoy?

____

____

____

____

____

What do I want my life to be like?

____

____

____

____

____

____

What was the most challenging obstacle that I conquered?

____

____

____

____

____

____

What accomplishment was I most proud of?

____

____

____

____

____

____

This is how my life has changed *After the Rain:*

In the bustling rhythm of life, daily meditations serve as sacred pauses—moments of stillness amidst the whirlwind of existence. Each morning or evening, as we close our eyes and delve into the silence, we are offered a respite from the relentless cacophony of the outer world. These meditative moments become bridges, connecting our conscious self to the vast reservoir of peace and wisdom within. As we breathe deeply, every inhalation draws in serenity, and every exhalation dispels the day's clutter and chaos.

Daily meditations become an intimate dialogue with the self, a space where thoughts and feelings are acknowledged, not judged. They cultivate mindfulness, grounding us in the present, and allowing the past's shadows and the future's uncertainties to melt away. In this haven of quietude, we are not just rejuvenating our minds but also forging a deeper connection with our inner essence. Over time, this daily ritual transforms from a mere practice to a life philosophy, instilling resilience, clarity, and an unwavering calm, equipping us to navigate the ebb and flow of life with grace and poise.

Daily Meditation

Today's Affirmation:

Today I'm feeling:

Today I promise myself that I will do the
following to move me closer to my goal(s).

Today's reflection:

Daily Meditation

Today's Affirmation:

Today I'm feeling:

Today I promise myself that I will do the
following to move me closer to my goal(s).

Today's reflection:

Daily Meditation

Today's Affirmation:

Today I'm feeling:

Today I promise myself that I will do the following to move me closer to my goal(s).

Today's reflection:

Daily Meditation

Today's Affirmation:

Today I'm feeling:

Today I promise myself that I will do the following to move me closer to my goal(s).

Today's reflection:

Daily Meditation

Today's Affirmation:

Today I'm feeling:

Today I promise myself that I will do the following to move me closer to my goal(s).

Today's reflection:

Daily Meditation

Today's Affirmation:

Today I'm feeling:

Today I promise myself that I will do the following to move me closer to my goal(s).

Today's reflection:

Daily Meditation

Today's Affirmation:

Today I'm feeling:

Today I promise myself that I will do the following to move me closer to my goal(s).

Today's reflection:

Daily Meditation

Today's Affirmation:

Today I'm feeling:

Today I promise myself that I will do the following to move me closer to my goal(s).

Today's reflection:

Daily Meditation

Today's Affirmation:

____

____

Today I'm feeling:

____

____

Today I promise myself that I will do the following to move me closer to my goal(s).

____

____

____

____

Today's reflection:

____

____

____

____

Daily Meditation

Today's Affirmation:

Today I'm feeling:

Today I promise myself that I will do the following to move me closer to my goal(s).

Today's reflection:

Daily Meditation

Today's Affirmation:

Today I'm feeling:

Today I promise myself that I will do the
following to move me closer to my goal(s).

Today's reflection:

Daily Meditation

Today's Affirmation:

Today I'm feeling:

Today I promise myself that I will do the
following to move me closer to my goal(s).

Today's reflection:

Daily Meditation

Today's Affirmation:

Today I'm feeling:

Today I promise myself that I will do the following to move me closer to my goal(s).

Today's reflection:

Daily Meditation

Today's Affirmation:

Today I'm feeling:

Today I promise myself that I will do the following to move me closer to my goal(s).

Today's reflection:

Daily Meditation

Today's Affirmation:

____

____

Today I'm feeling:

____

____

Today I promise myself that I will do the
following to move me closer to my goal(s).

____

____

____

Today's reflection:

____

____

____

Daily Meditation

Today's Affirmation:

Today I'm feeling:

Today I promise myself that I will do the
following to move me closer to my goal(s).

Today's reflection:

Daily Meditation

Today's Affirmation:

____

____

Today I'm feeling:

____

____

Today I promise myself that I will do the
following to move me closer to my goal(s).

____

____

____

____

Today's reflection:

____

____

____

Daily Meditation

Today's Affirmation:

____

____

Today I'm feeling:

____

____

Today I promise myself that I will do the following to move me closer to my goal(s).

____

____

____

Today's reflection:

____

____

____

Daily Meditation

Today's Affirmation:

____

____

Today I'm feeling:

____

____

Today I promise myself that I will do the following to move me closer to my goal(s).

____

____

____

____

Today's reflection:

____

____

____

____

Daily Meditation

Today's Affirmation:

____

____

Today I'm feeling:

____

____

Today I promise myself that I will do the
following to move me closer to my goal(s).

____

____

____

____

Today's reflection:

____

____

____

____

Daily Meditation

Today's Affirmation:

Today I'm feeling:

Today I promise myself that I will do the following to move me closer to my goal(s).

Today's reflection:

Daily Meditation

Today's Affirmation:

Today I'm feeling:

Today I promise myself that I will do the
following to move me closer to my goal(s).

Today's reflection:

Daily Meditation

Today's Affirmation:

____

____

Today I'm feeling:

____

____

Today I promise myself that I will do the
following to move me closer to my goal(s).

____

____

____

____

Today's reflection:

____

____

____

____

Daily Meditation

Today's Affirmation:

Today I'm feeling:

Today I promise myself that I will do the
following to move me closer to my goal(s).

Today's reflection:

Daily Meditation

Today's Affirmation:

Today I'm feeling:

Today I promise myself that I will do the following to move me closer to my goal(s).

Today's reflection:

Daily Meditation

Today's Affirmation:

____

____

Today I'm feeling:

____

____

Today I promise myself that I will do the following to move me closer to my goal(s).

____

____

____

Today's reflection:

____

____

____

Daily Meditation

Today's Affirmation:

Today I'm feeling:

Today I promise myself that I will do the following to move me closer to my goal(s).

Today's reflection:

Daily Meditation

Today's Affirmation:

Today I'm feeling:

Today I promise myself that I will do the following to move me closer to my goal(s).

Today's reflection:

Daily Meditation

Today's Affirmation:

Today I'm feeling:

Today I promise myself that I will do the following to move me closer to my goal(s).

Today's reflection:

Daily Meditation

Today's Affirmation:

Today I'm feeling:

Today I promise myself that I will do the following to move me closer to my goal(s).

Today's reflection:

Daily Meditation

Today's Affirmation:

Today I'm feeling:

Today I promise myself that I will do the following to move me closer to my goal(s).

Today's reflection:

Daily Meditation

Today's Affirmation:

Today I'm feeling:

Today I promise myself that I will do the following to move me closer to my goal(s).

Today's reflection:

Daily Meditation

Today's Affirmation:

Today I'm feeling:

Today I promise myself that I will do the following to move me closer to my goal(s).

Today's reflection:

Daily Meditation

Today's Affirmation:

Today I'm feeling:

Today I promise myself that I will do the
following to move me closer to my goal(s).

Today's reflection:

Daily Meditation

Today's Affirmation:

Today I'm feeling:

Today I promise myself that I will do the following to move me closer to my goal(s).

Today's reflection:

Daily Meditation

Today's Affirmation:

____

____

Today I'm feeling:

____

____

Today I promise myself that I will do the following to move me closer to my goal(s).

____

____

____

Today's reflection:

____

____

____

Daily Meditation

Today's Affirmation:

____

____

Today I'm feeling:

____

____

Today I promise myself that I will do the
following to move me closer to my goal(s).

____

____

____

Today's reflection:

____

____

____

Daily Meditation

Today's Affirmation:

____

____

Today I'm feeling:

____

____

Today I promise myself that I will do the
following to move me closer to my goal(s).

____

____

____

____

Today's reflection:

____

____

____

Daily Meditation

Today's Affirmation:

Today I'm feeling:

Today I promise myself that I will do the following to move me closer to my goal(s).

Today's reflection:

Daily Meditation

Today's Affirmation:

____

____

Today I'm feeling:

____

____

Today I promise myself that I will do the
following to move me closer to my goal(s).

____

____

____

Today's reflection:

____

____

____

Daily Meditation

Today's Affirmation:

Today I'm feeling:

Today I promise myself that I will do the following to move me closer to my goal(s).

Today's reflection:

Daily Meditation

Today's Affirmation:

____

____

Today I'm feeling:

____

____

Today I promise myself that I will do the
following to move me closer to my goal(s).

____

____

____

Today's reflection:

____

____

____

Daily Meditation

Today's Affirmation:

Today I'm feeling:

Today I promise myself that I will do the following to move me closer to my goal(s).

Today's reflection:

Daily Meditation

Today's Affirmation:

Today I'm feeling:

Today I promise myself that I will do the
following to move me closer to my goal(s).

Today's reflection:

Daily Meditation

Today's Affirmation:

Today I'm feeling:

Today I promise myself that I will do the
following to move me closer to my goal(s).

Today's reflection:

Daily Meditation

Today's Affirmation:

____

____

Today I'm feeling:

____

____

Today I promise myself that I will do the following to move me closer to my goal(s).

____

____

____

Today's reflection:

____

____

____

Daily Meditation

Today's Affirmation:

____

____

Today I'm feeling:

____

____

Today I promise myself that I will do the following to move me closer to my goal(s).

____

____

____

____

Today's reflection:

____

____

____

Daily Meditation

Today's Affirmation:

Today I'm feeling:

Today I promise myself that I will do the following to move me closer to my goal(s).

Today's reflection:

Daily Meditation

Today's Affirmation:

____

____

Today I'm feeling:

____

____

Today I promise myself that I will do the following to move me closer to my goal(s).

____

____

____

____

Today's reflection:

____

____

____

Daily Meditation

Today's Affirmation:

Today I'm feeling:

Today I promise myself that I will do the
following to move me closer to my goal(s).

Today's reflection:

Daily Meditation

Today's Affirmation:

Today I'm feeling:

Today I promise myself that I will do the following to move me closer to my goal(s).

Today's reflection:

Daily Meditation

Today's Affirmation:

Today I'm feeling:

Today I promise myself that I will do the following to move me closer to my goal(s).

Today's reflection:

Daily Meditation

Today's Affirmation:

____

____

Today I'm feeling:

____

____

Today I promise myself that I will do the following to move me closer to my goal(s).

____

____

____

Today's reflection:

____

____

____

Daily Meditation

Today's Affirmation:

____

____

Today I'm feeling:

____

____

Today I promise myself that I will do the
following to move me closer to my goal(s).

____

____

____

Today's reflection:

____

____

____

Daily Meditation

Today's Affirmation:

Today I'm feeling:

Today I promise myself that I will do the following to move me closer to my goal(s).

Today's reflection:

Daily Meditation

Today's Affirmation:

Today I'm feeling:

Today I promise myself that I will do the following to move me closer to my goal(s).

Today's reflection:

Daily Meditation

Today's Affirmation:

Today I'm feeling:

Today I promise myself that I will do the following to move me closer to my goal(s).

Today's reflection:

Daily Meditation

Today's Affirmation:

____

____

Today I'm feeling:

____

____

Today I promise myself that I will do the
following to move me closer to my goal(s).

____

____

____

Today's reflection:

____

____

____

Daily Meditation

Today's Affirmation:

____

____

Today I'm feeling:

____

____

Today I promise myself that I will do the following to move me closer to my goal(s).

____

____

____

____

Today's reflection:

____

____

____

____

Daily Meditation

Today's Affirmation:

Today I'm feeling:

Today I promise myself that I will do the
following to move me closer to my goal(s).

Today's reflection:

Daily Meditation

Today's Affirmation:

____

____

Today I'm feeling:

____

____

Today I promise myself that I will do the
following to move me closer to my goal(s).

____

____

____

Today's reflection:

____

____

____

Daily Meditation

Today's Affirmation:

____

____

Today I'm feeling:

____

____

Today I promise myself that I will do the following to move me closer to my goal(s).

____

____

____

____

Today's reflection:

____

____

____

Daily Meditation

Today's Affirmation:

____

____

Today I'm feeling:

____

____

Today I promise myself that I will do the following to move me closer to my goal(s).

____

____

____

Today's reflection:

____

____

____

Reflection is a soulful dance between the heart and the pen, where thoughts and emotions pirouette across the pages in intimate choreography. Each entry becomes a sanctified space, a rendezvous between the present self and the myriad versions that have existed in days gone by. In the act of writing, we don't just recount experiences; we delve deeper, extracting nuances, unveiling patterns, and often, discovering facets of ourselves previously uncharted.

As the ink flows, it carries with it a cleansing. Triumphs are celebrated, regrets are confronted, and sorrows find solace. The paper absorbs not just words but also the weight of emotions, acting as a silent confidant, never judging, always listening. Over time, these pages become a tapestry of life, woven with threads of memories, insights, dreams, and revelations.

But the magic of reflective journaling isn't confined to introspection alone. As we revisit old entries, we often find wisdom waiting to be unearthed. Moments once perceived as insignificant reveal their profound impact, while certain challenges, once insurmountable, now appear as milestones of growth. This cyclical dialogue with our past enables a clearer vision for the future, providing guidance, clarity, and a sense of purpose.

In a world swamped with external noise, a reflective journal becomes an oasis of authenticity. It's a sanctuary where masks are shed, and souls are born. The act of writing, vulnerable and unfiltered, reminds us of our humanity, our imperfections, and our innate potential for growth. As days turn into years, this journal stands as a testament to life's journey, each page echoing the beauty of evolution, resilience, and the undying quest for self-awareness. In the sacred act of reflective journaling, we don't just document life; we converse with existence itself.

Reflections

Reflections

Reflections

Reflections

Reflections

Reflections

Reflections

Reflections

Reflections

Reflections

Reflections

Reflections

Reflections

Reflections

We can't control when the storms of life will appear or forecast how long they will last. But, we can prepare and protect ourselves to reduce the impact of the storms while understanding their purpose.

As you continue your life's journey, you will encounter rain again, some drizzles and some thunderstorms, but never allow the rain to wash away your dreams, goals and desires for success in love and life.

Here are a few additional tips that you can use to help you weather the storms of life. Don't wait until **After the Rain** is over to live; smile and dance during the rain, don't just endure it. Remember self-care is essential.

- Find a support group
- Connect with an accountability partner
- Spend quiet time alone reflecting
- Develop a success log

About the Author

Deondriea is an accomplished confidence and transitional life coach, award-winning author, and dynamic speaker. Deondriea empowers individuals to break free from their comfort zones and transcend self-imposed fears as she guides individuals on transformative journeys to unearth and embrace their inner confidence. Her passion lies in guiding others towards personal growth, development, and transformation.

Deondriea's journey began with her own personal experiences of overcoming adversity and self-doubt. Through introspection and a deep understanding of the human psyche, she discovered the power of confidence and the tremendous impact it can have on an individual's life. Motivated by her own transformative journey, she made it her mission to inspire and motivate others to unleash their full potential.

Other Books by Deondriea

Access Granted: Unlock Your Confidence to Unlock the Life You Desire.

Access Granted: The Guided Journal

Cultivating Confidence

You! Branding Yourself for Success

Coach with Deondriea: Embark on a Journey of Transformation with Deondriea as Your Guide!

www.deondriea.com